PASSENGER SHIP

Hannah Jacobs

Hamish Hamilton
London

Acknowledgments

The author and publishers would like to thank Cunard Line and the crew of the *QE2* for their assistance during the production of this book. Special thanks go to Eric Flounders, Public Relations Manager, Richard Place, Purchasing Manager, and Peter Mullington, Social Director on board the *QE2*.

The photograph on the front cover is reproduced with the permission of Cunard Line.

First published in Great Britain 1987 by
Hamish Hamilton Children's Books
27 Wrights Lane, London W8 5TZ
Copyright © 1987 by Hannah Jacobs
Copyright (illustrations) © 1987 by Chris Fairclough

Design by Miriam Yarrien
Artwork by Tony Garrett

British Library Cataloguing in Publication Data
Jacobs, Hannah
Passenger ship.
1. Passenger ships—Juvenile literature
I. Title
623.8′243   VM381

ISBN 0–241–11880–8

Typeset by Katerprint Typesetting Services, Oxford

Contents

Introduction

It is 7 o'clock on a cold, grey morning in Southampton. In the town, people are just getting up, or starting on their way to work. But at the quayside, gangs of dock workers have been busy since dawn. The passenger ship, the *Queen Elizabeth 2*, arrived from New York during the night and now fresh supplies are being loaded for her next trip in twelve hours' time.

The *Queen Elizabeth 2* is perhaps the most famous passenger ship in the world. She was built in 1967 and, unlike nearly all previous transatlantic passenger ships, was purposely designed to undertake pleasure cruises. She was officially launched in 1969, and ever since then has been classed as one of the most luxurious liners afloat. Every year, thousands of people pay top prices to sample one of her many cruises — from a three-day jaunt down the English Channel, to a three-month cruise around the world.

A luxurious holiday at sea is a fairly new idea in the travel business, but one which is rapidly growing in popularity. Before aeroplanes were brought into general use, ships were an essential means of long distance transportation — at first, mainly for mail, and then for people too. Until as late as 1960, the numbers of passengers travelling by sea and air were roughly equal. But only five years later, the situation was very different. By this time, the proportion of sea travellers had slumped to 14%, a potentially disastrous situation for all shipping lines. They realised that unless something drastic was done, many would go out of business.

Shipping firms such as Cunard decided that the best solution was to try and change the image of the passenger liner. It was obvious that ships would never be able to compete with aeroplanes in terms of speed. But they could offer a much higher standard of comfort and elegance — in other words, a relaxing holiday away from all the worries and tensions of everyday living. Taking this idea further, Cunard started to plan a new kind of ship, which would combine all the advantages of a first-class hotel with the attractions of a sea voyage. They decided to open out all the public areas on the ship, and so abandon nearly all class distinctions between passengers. They also decided to replace the usual small windows with blinds,

8

fitted to disguise the fact that passengers were at sea, with enormous picture windows running the length of the ship. Many other changes followed.

And so Cunard — who had originally started business in 1840 running a transatlantic mail delivery service between England and America — started to build the *QE2*. By 1965, the first section of the keel had been laid at John Brown's shipyard on the River Clyde in Scotland. Just over two years later, after a variety of teething problems, she was launched by Her Majesty Queen Elizabeth II.

Food supplies are loaded onto the *QE2*.

1
Planning a cruise

Shortly after the *QE2* arrives in Southampton, her home port, the dock workers start loading the food supplies needed for the next voyage. Nowadays, the ship rarely stays in port for longer than twelve hours, so no time must be lost. Most of the supplies are loaded via four narrow gangways spaced at regular intervals down the length of the ship. These gangways lead on to Four and Five decks. Different types of goods are loaded at each gangway.

Gangway 1, nearest the front (for'ard) of the ship, is used mainly for fresh fruit and vegetables. Much of it is supplied by local green-grocers, with the rest being delivered from New Covent Garden Market in London. The choice of produce depends in part on when the cruise takes place. For example, in summer soft fruits such as raspberries and strawberries are much more plentiful than at other times of the year. However, even in winter, the ship carries a wide variety of fruits and vegetables, both home-grown and imported.

The choice of supplier depends on quality and price. The contractor who can deliver the highest quality goods at the lowest price generally wins the order. But if prices are equal the order is normally given to a supplier nearby, who is more likely to deliver on time. In return, local greengrocers do their best to give good service so that valuable business will not be taken from them and given to their competitors.

The fresh produce is delivered to the quay in the early morning. The dock workers carefully lift the boxes out of the vans and lorries and load them one by one onto a small conveyor belt. They take care that nothing is bruised or squashed. At the other end of the conveyor, the kitchen hands carry the boxes into the store rooms.

Gangway 2 is mainly used for tinned and frozen foods, and gangways 3 and 4 for deep-frozen meat and fish. As all these goods last much longer than fresh fruit and vegetables, they can be selected several months before they will be eaten. They can also be transported long distances without going bad. As a result, Cunard

10

spends a considerable amount of time and care choosing the best supplier for each product. Thus, the tinned carrots are imported from France; the salmon is sent from Scotland and Norway; and the caviar is imported from Russia.

Most wines, spirits and soft drinks are loaded for'ard. The bottles are carefully packed into special metal containers and lifted gently aboard by crane. A huge trapdoor on each deck opens to allow the containers to be lowered safely down onto Eight deck. Thousands of litres of beer are pumped straight from quayside tankers into enormous stainless steel tanks. From here, there is a direct supply to the bars on the ship.

Supplies of all food and drink items are the responsibility of the Cunard supply manager in Southampton. At the beginning of each year, he gives the suppliers an estimate of the quantities that will be required, and a delivery schedule for the next twelve months. After several years' experience it becomes fairly simple to calculate the amounts of food and drink that will be required. The suppliers are then selected for price, quality and service, and contracts are agreed. These contracts are usually binding until the end of the year

Fresh fruit and vegetables are lifted carefully onto a conveyor belt.

11

so long as the suppliers keep to the expected high standard. For the most part, the more experienced suppliers win the contracts. The quality of their products is known to be high, their service reliable and their prices competitive. Companies chosen as suppliers regard their connection with Cunard as a valuable advertisement to gain other contracts and do their very best to make sure nothing endangers it.

For the world cruise, suppliers are appointed at least three months in advance. After consultation with the ship, orders are placed in good time to ensure that the right quality goods are available on arrival in ports such as Sydney, Auckland, Hong Kong and Singapore.

Maintaining the reputation of the *QE2* is of prime importance to her owners. Should it slip, business would soon suffer. As a result, continuous efforts are made to improve standards throughout the ship. Every few years, the design of all the crockery and glassware is updated. Here you can see the purchasing manager looking at a new range of crockery to be used in the restaurants. The manufacturer claims the china combines elegance with strength, an important factor as breakages on board ship can quickly become unacceptably high. His is one of several designs submitted to Cunard. As the ship carries nearly 70,000 items of crockery altogether, a variety of manufacturers are competing for the order. This enables Cunard to negotiate lower prices. As in all other areas, the company aims to marry the highest possible quality with the lowest possible price.

Cunard's Purchasing Manager inspects new crockery designs for the ship.

2
On board

Towards mid afternoon, crew members who have been given shore leave return to the ship. It is time to prepare for the passengers' arrival in a couple of hours' time. The stewards and stewardesses check the cabins to make sure everything is neat and tidy; the chefs begin cooking the evening meal; and the bar staff fetch extra supplies from the store rooms below.

At 4 o'clock, the first passengers walk down the gangway and onto the ship. They are welcomed by a jazz band playing popular tunes from the latest hit shows. A photographer takes their picture. The stewardesses look at everyone's ticket and explains where the cabins are to be found. All the luggage is still on the quay, waiting for an army of porters to carry it on board.

Passengers are greeted by
QE2 staff.

The passengers stream onto the ship, cheerful and excited. For many, this is the beginning of a dream come true; others are simply pleased to be starting another holiday on the QE2. A steady flow of people sets off in search of their cabins. As there are ten passenger decks altogether, this is not as easy as it sounds! All over the ship, groups of lost people stare up at direction signs and try to work out where they are. Some will never succeed in understanding the ship's layout. For them, each outing away from their cabin becomes a test of memory and nerves.

Inside all the cabins, the passengers discover a note of welcome from their steward and stewardess, a programme of the day's events, and a small arrangement of flowers. The cabins themselves vary according to price. Unlike some other cruise liners, the *QE2* does not divide passengers into separate classes — apart from providing first-class restaurants and lounges for those paying top prices. Instead, everyone is admitted into all the public rooms, and the cabins are divided into sixteen 'grades' — ranging from an inside room with four bunk beds and shower in grade N, to a luxury room with double bed, verandah and bath in grade AA. Depending on the type and length of cruise, the top grade is approximately four times more expensive than the lowest.

Whatever the grade of cabin, its occupants are allocated a steward and stewardess for the duration of the cruise. It is their job to tidy

Cabins are thoroughly cleaned each day.

14

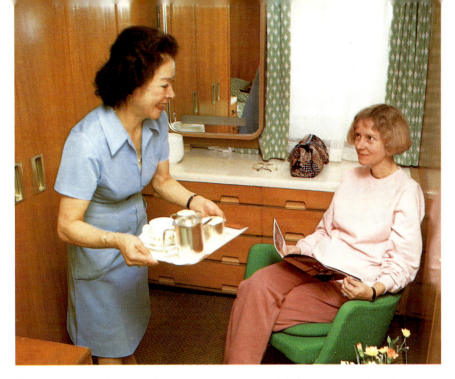

QE2 staff call 'British cruises' "teacup cruises".

the cabin each morning, to serve any drinks or snacks the passengers may want, and to make sure the corridor walls and carpet are kept clean. Each steward and stewardess looks after an average of eleven cabins between them.

Like most of the crew, the cabin staff work very hard. Nearly every day, they are on duty for ten hours, with a three-hour break in the afternoon. When the ship is in port, they are often given only a few hours ashore, and sometimes not even that. The *QE2* spends so little time in port nowadays that time off for the staff has become increasingly limited.

If passengers want to call a steward or stewardess to their cabin, they press one of two calling buttons. A buzzer sounds inside the nearest 'pantry' (a kind of large kitchen and store room combined), and a light goes on in the corridor outside their cabin. This tells the cabin staff which cabin to go to. Once the order has been taken, the light is switched off by hand. Orders are prepared in the pantry; there are three of four pantries to each deck. If food and drinks had to be fetched from the main kitchens, they would be cold by the time they were served. But in a pantry, staff can prepare anything from a cup of coffee to an elaborate late night supper. Most orders on a cruise starting from Southampton are for a pot of tea. For this reason, staff have nicknamed 'British' cruises, "teacup cruises"!

15

3
In the kitchens

At full stretch, the *QE2* can carry up to 1850 passengers and 995 crew — a total of almost 3000 people. All of them must be fed, and the passengers at least expect a high standard of food and wine. To satisfy this demand, the ship is equipped with three separate kitchens and well over a hundred chefs.

The three kitchens serve four different dining-rooms — the Queens Grill, Princess Grill and the Columbia (reserved for first-class passengers only), and the Tables of the World. The largest kitchen serves the Columbia restaurant and the Princess Grill and has an area of nearly 1400 square metres. Here, dozens of cooks produce up to 782 meals three times a day, as well as a lavish midnight buffet every evening. It also supplies thousands of rolls, croissants and sweetmeats.

The bakers are among the hardest working staff on the ship. Their day starts at 5 a.m., when they begin to prepare the 3000 or so rolls, croissants and Danish pastries needed for breakfast. All the breads and cakes are baked fresh each morning, although any leftover *petit fours* (small fancy cakes) may be stored overnight. The bakers and confectioners (who make the cakes, gateaux, sweets and puddings) use the same white flour for most of their baking. But they also have two or three different types of brown flour, which they make into wholemeal bread or rolls, or use for people on special diets. The loaves are baked in a huge oven fitted with long shelves. The shelves slowly circulate inside the oven so that they are baked evenly all the way through. Once breakfast is over, more rolls are baked for lunch, dinner and the buffet. Work usually ends at about six or seven o'clock at night.

Like the bakers, the nine confectioners have to produce certain items each day. These include nearly 6000 pieces of cake for afternoon tea (on the British cruises) and 5000 *petit fours* for the evening buffet. The latter are particularly popular with American passengers who tend to have a sweeter tooth than the British. In

Over 3000 rolls, croissants and pastries are baked each morning.

Putting the final touches to some *petits fours*.

addition, they have to bake a variety of puddings and gateaux for each day's meals. These are chosen by the executive chef, who pins up each day's menus in the kitchens two or three days before they appear in the restaurants.

At about 7 a.m., the soup chefs report for work. They make all the soups and stews for the restaurant, amounting to nearly 2000 litres a day. The chefs have to start early because most of the ingredients for the soups are fresh, and have to be cut up or sliced before

17

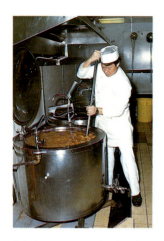

Stirring soup can be hard work!

Preparing a white sauce.

cooking. The chopped vegetables (or cubes of meat, poultry or fish) are then tipped into huge stainless steel vats, the largest of which holds up to nearly 400 litres of liquid at one time. The stock is poured in, and the mixture gently heated until it blends into soup. At intervals, the soup is stirred with enormous spoons a metre or more in length.

Preparation of the day's main courses starts as most of the passengers are finishing breakfast. As for other sections of the menu, there are special chefs to cook the meat, fish and vegetables, and each group works in a separate part of the kitchen. For both lunch and dinner, there are normally four hot meat dishes and two hot fish dishes, all of which are served with a selection of vegetables. No dish is ever offered more than once a day.

Under the watchful eye of a senior chef, the men start work. (There are no female chefs on board.) Although most of the chefs have worked on ship for a year or more, there are always a few newcomers, and they need supervision and training. But the more experienced chefs often have little time to explain things in detail, and the young cooks frequently have to rely on observation and common sense. Some, who may be away from home for the first time, discover the job is not to their taste. Instead of sailing around the world, visiting exotic new countries, they find themselves working long hours in a windowless kitchen. They may feel seasick, lonely and tired. A few decide to give up and go home, sometimes in the middle of a cruise. The executive chef then has to spread their jobs among the other chefs in the group — so making their work load even heavier than usual.

Bad weather can also cause problems in the kitchen. On the North Atlantic route in particular (between Southampton and New York), the sea can be very rough. In winter, it is not unusual for the ship to be caught in winds of force 8 or 9 and waves more than 5 metres high. On these occasions, it becomes extremely difficult to produce any meals at all. Bowls and utensils can skid across the working surfaces, soup slops onto the floor, and cream cakes collide into each other and get squashed. Fortunately, far fewer passengers than usual turn up for meals! This is one reason why there are no transatlantic crossings between January and April.

Nearly all the ship's meat and fish is deep-frozen until needed. Otherwise, it would quickly go bad. A day or two before some meat

18

is to be cooked, it is taken out of the huge freezer rooms and left to thaw. When it has completely thawed, the store room butchers cut it into manageable pieces. If they are told exactly how the meat is to be cooked, they cut the portions very precisely. Then all the kitchen butchers need do is the final trimming. The butcher's job is made particularly difficult in bad weather because the meat has to be cut with a very sharp knife. When the ship is rolling, the knife can easily slip. It is not unusual for one of the patients in the ship's hospital to be a butcher with a cut finger.

A lot of care and attention is also taken with the presentation of food. The chefs know that much of the enjoyment of a meal depends on its appearance. A few chefs are specially skilled at decorating food — so much so that they can almost be called food artists. Some of the most elaborately decorated food on the *QE2* is prepared for the midnight buffet. This is held every night in the Columbia restaurant, and is particularly popular with passengers who have eaten an early dinner. In this picture, a chef is putting the finishing touches to a Chinese pagoda carved entirely out of butter. It has taken many hours to complete. Beside the pagoda is an enormous cold ham decorated with tomatoes, peppers and olives.

Each section of the kitchen is run by a head chef, who in turn is responsible to the executive chef. It is the head chef's job to check that his section is working smoothly, and that the standard of cooking remains high. Part of his job involves making sure that the chefs do not run out of supplies. When he notices that stocks are running low, he reports the shortage to the executive chef, who orders whatever is needed from the store rooms below. The executive chef records exactly how much food and drink is consumed during each cruise so that, at the end of the year, he and the supply manager on shore know how much to order for the following year. The table below shows how much food is eaten during a typical 11-day round trip from Southampton to New York.

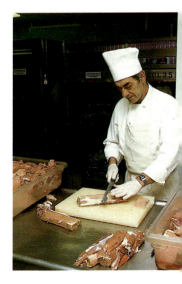

Trimming the fat off meat for today's lunch.

Carving a pagoda out of butter.

7112 Kgs Beef	45 Kgs Caviar
3048 Kgs Lamb	10,160 Kgs Potatoes
1524 Kgs Pork	9144 Kgs Fresh Vegetables
2794 Kgs Chicken	6096 Kgs Frozen Vegetables
1524 Kgs Turkey	7260 Kgs Fruit
3048 Kgs Bacon and Ham	2032 Kgs Butter

3048 Kgs Fish	160 Cartons Eggs
680 Kgs Lobster	3409 Litres Ice Cream
227 Kgs Crab	2273 Litres Cream
272 Kgs Salmon	12,274 Litres Milk
	2540 Kgs Sugar

Another important part of the executive chef's job is to maintain standards of hygiene in the kitchens. This is no easy task when there are so many people working in a fairly small area; during the busiest periods of the day, there is no time to mop up spillages. But after every meal, all the work surfaces, stoves, and floors are thoroughly cleaned before the next shift starts. Several times a year, the kitchens are inspected by both the British and American health authorities to ensure they are up to standard. The inspectors also check that all equipment complies with their country's health and safety regulations. If something is faulty, it has to be changed immediately.

By far the most important part of the executive chef's job is to plan each day's menus. This is normally done at least ten days in advance. The menus are then given to the section heads, who make sure they have all the necessary ingredients. On short cruises, it is relatively simple to provide a variety of dishes, but on longer cruises (particularly the world cruise) the chef has to be careful not to repeat meals too often. Passengers would soon complain if a pattern began to emerge.

The executive chef is also responsible for planning special menus for celebrations during the year. Even at Christmas, when everyone expects roast turkey and Christmas pudding, he still has to invent something extra-delicious for the starter and first course. And there are always people who don't like the traditional fare, and must be offered an interesting alternative.

Other people may need a different menu for reasons of health or religion. For them, there are gluten-free, salt-free and kosher foods on request. Meals for orthodox Jews are cooked in a separate kosher kitchen staffed by Jewish cooks, who prepare everything in accordance with Jewish food laws.

4
The store rooms

The store rooms are on Seven and Eight decks. Seven deck is used for all dried goods, fresh fruit and vegetables, and any meat or fish to be cooked within the next few days. Eight deck is used for deep-frozen meat and fish, and for all bottled and canned drinks. Towards the bow, there are twenty-seven beer vats, containing a maximum of nearly 60,000 litres.

The dried goods store looks rather like a small supermarket. Rows and rows of shelves run down the length of the room loaded with jams, sugar, mustard, flour — and many other things besides. As stocks in a kitchen run low, a junior is sent downstairs to collect whatever is wanted. If there is a lot, he loads everything into a trolley and uses the lift to take it back upstairs. The store-keeper makes a note of what has been removed and records each amount on the store room computer. In this way, he can easily keep track of how much is being used.

The dried goods store.

Additional supplies are stacked in cardboard boxes around the walls. From here, they are gradually transferred onto the shelves. When a new delivery is loaded on board, the store keeper makes sure that any remaining goods go to the top of the pile. In this way, even the slower-moving items are unlikely to go bad. Of all the hundreds of foods in the store, the fastest mover is baked beans. These are served to the crew only.

Any food which remains fresh for only a short time has to be stored in cool rooms, or freezer rooms. The choice of room depends on the type of food being stored. Foods such as fresh fruit and vegetables, eggs, milk and cheese cannot be frozen or they will become inedible. But meat and fish can be deep-frozen for weeks and still lose very little of their original flavour and texture when cooked.

The cool rooms vary in size. One of the smallest is used for storing cheese. Over thirty kinds of cheese are kept here from several different countries. Some cheeses can be kept indefinitely; others

21

Inspecting cheeses.

become stale or over-ripe after a limited period of time. The store keeper has to check them regularly to make sure they are in peak condition.

The fruit and vegetables are kept in a much larger room farther along the corridor. Most fruit and vegetables stay fresh for only a few days, even inside a cold room. This means that on a cruise lasting a week or more, further supplies must be brought on board at regular intervals. Obviously, some ports are better able to do this than others. So when a long cruise is being planned, one of the factors that has to be taken into consideration is the need to find a series of ports which can provide a suitable range of fresh foods at reasonable prices. Once a decision has been made, the supply manager contacts these ports to arrange the supply and delivery. Sometimes, he flies to key ports ahead of the *QE2* to make sure everything goes smoothly. When the ship is only in port for twelve hours at a time, it is crucial everything is delivered on time.

The cold rooms for the meat and poultry stretch almost the width

Fresh fruit and vegetables can only be stored for a few days.

22

of the ship. Inside it is −10 degrees centigrade, cold enough to kill anyone trapped inside for longer than twelve hours. In order to avoid any accidents, there is an alarm bell inside each room in case the doors shut by mistake. Here, the once deep-frozen meat is left to thaw before it is cut, trimmed, and taken up to the kitchens. As so much meat is used at a time, it is transported in large stainless steel trolleys, and then left in plastic boxes loaded onto steel shelves. The boxes are arranged in date order. An average of 850 kilograms of fillet beef is eaten at each main meal.

On a long cruise, there is so much meat that some of it has to be stored at the very bottom of the ship, on Eight deck. Here, too, are stored all the wines, beers, spirits and soft drinks. They are put here because Eight deck is below sea level, and therefore the most stable part of the ship. Wines and beers should be shaken as little as possible, or they soon become undrinkable. At the start of a world cruise, the ship is loaded with over 20,000 bottles of wine and a quarter of a million cans of soft drinks.

Deep frozen meat and poultry is delivered to the cold rooms.

23

5
The engine room

When plans were being drawn up for the building of the *QE2*, one of the planners' main aims was to design a ship which was as powerful as she was luxurious. She should not only be able to cross any sea in the world, but do so with a speed and manoeuvrability previously unknown. Nowadays, although the engine room has had several major refits, the *QE2* is still considered one of the most technically advanced passenger ships afloat.

Despite its name, the engine room is not just one room but several enormous, high-ceilinged areas housing a variety of giant machines. They are found on Seven and Eight decks. Nearby, there are a number of small workshops where minor repairs and improvements are carried out.

Part of the engine room.

24

Power for the ship is generated by three huge boilers, each weighing 282,261 kgs. When fitted in 1967, they were the largest boilers ever installed on a ship. The steam from the boilers drives two high, and two low-pressure turbines which supply the power to turn the two propeller shafts. The shafts run along the port (left, as you face the bows) and starboard (right) of the ship. They are each 76 metres long and approximately 60 centimetres in diameter. Like all the other pieces of machinery in the engine room, the shafts are regularly cleaned and polished. This stops any dirt clogging the works or damaging the steel.

In heavy seas, ships are forced to slow down. So to avoid losing more speed than necessary, the *QE2* is equipped with four stabiliser fins. These are triangular sheets of steel, each covering an area of about $6\frac{1}{2}$ square metres. Most of the time, they are folded inside the ship's hull. But if the sea gets rough, the chief engineer (on instructions from the bridge) operates a switch to bring them forward. Once fully extended, they automatically change position to counter the movement and direction of the sea's swell, and help stop the ship rolling. Without them, the *QE2* would arrive late much more often than she does — and her passengers would be seasick much more frequently than they are!

All the electricity for the ship is supplied by three huge alternators. Each one is capable of producing $5\frac{1}{2}$ million kilowatts of power. Think of the beam from an ordinary 100 watt light bulb at home and you will realise how powerful this is. The alternators are in a large, brightly lit area next to the main control room. It is very hot and noisy here, and the engineers wear light clothes and protective ear muffs. They are only allowed to work for three hours at a time. Usually, only two alternators are used at a time, so allowing the third to be checked and serviced. The only time they are all shut down is when the ship is in dry dock for her annual refit.

The engine room also contains many other machines. One is the reverse osmosis plant. This takes sea water on board and purifies it so that it is safe for drinking. The plant purifies 1,219,260 kgs of sea water a day. There is also a sewage plant, circulating pumps for the cooling system, and an air conditioning plant, a vital 'extra' for cruises to the tropics.

All this machinery is carefully monitored from the main control room. Here, sensitive equipment automatically registers how much

Cleaning a propeller shaft.

The main control room.

power is being used in any one area. If a machine were to overload, warning lights would flash and an alarm would sound. Long before this, however, an engineer would almost certainly have noticed a fault on one of the closed-circuit TV screens. There are always at least six engineers on duty, day or night.

Even so, there are repairs to be done. The *QE2* is now over twenty years old, and has had a hard-working life, including several weeks in the South Atlantic during the Falklands War in 1982. However well she is looked after, different sections crack under the strain. As many repairs as possible are done at sea. The ship's workshops are well equipped, and the mechanics used to coping with a variety of problems. Major repairs have to wait until the ship is in dry dock.

In recent years, the *QE2* has spent less and less time in port between the end of one cruise and the beginning of the next. There are two main reasons for this. First, the cost of running a passenger ship is now so high that the *QE2* cannot afford to be idle for longer than necessary. The fewer cruises she undertakes, the less income she earns. Second, the charge for tying up in dock is so expensive everywhere that each extra hour in port reduces profits. As a result, the *QE2* rarely spends more than twelve hours between cruises (this is sometimes reduced to five in New York), except for a month in winter when she undergoes her annual refit.

6
The bridge

High up on Signal deck, nearly 40 metres above the water line, is the bridge. This is where all the navigational equipment and safety controls are located. The bridge spans the width of the ship, so giving the navigating officers an uninterrupted view on all sides.

The *QE2*'s bridge consists of two main areas, known as 'the front of line' and 'the back of line'. Most of the navigational equipment is at the front, directly below an enormous window overlooking the bow. At one time, ships were steered with a wheel, rather like cars are today. But now, most of the steering is automatic. The only time when the wheel is still regularly used is during periods of heavy traffic, or when the ship is going in and out of port.

Above, A navigating officer surveys the horizon.

Right, 'The front of line'.

Out at sea, the officers use advanced radar and navigational equipment to check the *QE2*'s exact position and to make sure her way forward is clear. A recent addition is the collision avoidance system. This not only shows where any oncoming ships are, but works out their course, speed and direction. It takes only three minutes to do this for each ship, and it can cope with up to twenty ships at a time.

Another recent addition is a satellite navigator, the first to be fitted on a passenger ship. This sophisticated piece of equipment is linked up to various satellites orbiting the earth, which plot the position of the *QE2* at intervals of 35 to 100 minutes. The readings are accurate to within 100 metres, a huge improvement on more traditional methods of location.

But no matter how advanced the equipment is, the *QE2* continues to carry up to date charts of all the major, and many of the minor, coastlines and waterways of the world. These are stored behind line. Nowadays, they are mainly used for planning future cruises. But were any pieces of navigational equipment to break down, the officers would have to rely on them until the fault was repaired. All Masters (officers who are qualified to take charge of a ship) are trained to use both traditional and advanced methods of navigation.

The itineraries for each year's cruises are completed at least twelve months in advance. The planning starts on the bridge, and normally the first cruise to be considered is the annual world cruise

Maps and charts are used mainly for planning future cruises.

which lasts from January to April. This is the most important voyage in the ship's diary; it is the longest, the most profitable, and the most complicated to arrange. It also attracts a large number of regulars, so each trip must be substantially different from the last, yet still include ports of interest to sightseers. Equally, it is important that these ports can supply suitable additional foods, are not too expensive, and are not politically unstable. Not surprisingly, it can take several months before every detail is finalised. Other regular cruises include two and three-week trips to the Caribbean, five-day transatlantic cruises, and a variety of short European cruises.

As the control centre of the ship, the bridge is in close communication with the engine room and other key areas of the QE2. Most conversations between the bridge and engine room take place on a direct link telephone. The telephone has its own electricity supply so that contact can be maintained in an emergency. But official orders are given by means of a panel of labelled buttons, which light up according to the instruction given. There is an identical panel in the engine room's main control room. Thus when a button is pressed on the bridge, the equivalent button in the control room instantly lights up. The engineer immediately knows what is required, and errors and misunderstandings are cut to a minimum.

The bridge is ultimately responsible for the safety of the ship, its passengers and its crew. It is therefore in charge of all safety controls, alarms and emergency lights. If there is a possibility that the ship may have to be abandoned, it is also the bridge's responsibility to direct passengers and crew to the boat stations. A boat station is a gathering point for a pre-arranged number of people in an emergency. A maximum of 200 people is allocated to each boat station. Once assembled, the different groups may be directed to the lifeboats. In order to make sure all passengers know which station they should go to, there is always a boat drill soon after embarkation. During this drill, everyone learns to recognise the alarm and to put on their lifejackets correctly.

Given the crucial importance of the bridge, it is not surprising that great care is taken to make it as secure as possible. As a result, there is only one staircase up to the bridge, and only one entrance door, which has to be opened from the inside. A 24-hour closed-circuit TV shows officers on duty who is arriving and who is leaving. Only a few specially authorised crew are normally allowed access.

7
Back-up services

The radio room

The jobs done by some sections of the ship may not be as crucial as those already described, but they are nevertheless very important. Perhaps the most essential is that carried out by the radio room.

The radio room is situated on Boat deck and, like other key areas of the ship, is manned twenty-four hours a day. Its main function is to help maintain and promote safety at sea. To this end, the officers on duty are in constant contact with the outside world, by means of radio telegraphy, telex machines, and satellite communications. All outward calls are prefaced with the *QE2*'s own call sign, GBTT. In this way, any ship in the world immediately knows where the call is coming from. Each hour, there are several 3-minute periods of silence, during which time no radio messages are sent by any ship. This is to ensure that if a distress call is being sent, it can be picked up and acted upon.

Inside the radio room.

The hospital

With a possible total of nearly 3000 people on board, there is almost always someone who falls ill or is injured during a cruise. Medical complaints vary from a simple case of seasickness, to a sudden emergency requiring immediate treatment. But apart from exceptional cases, the *QE2* has the staff and the facilities to cope with both.

The hospital is situated on Six deck, near the waterline, where the movement of the ship is less noticeable than on higher decks. It is also close to several working areas of the ship, so enabling the crew to get there quickly and easily. This is important because all crew are given regular check-ups to make sure they are healthy. Standards are quite strict. Anyone who is overweight, for example, is sent ashore until the extra kilograms have been lost. From time to time, the entire crew has to be injected against dangerous diseases they might otherwise catch in certain parts of the world.

When someone does fall ill, whether crew or passenger, he or she

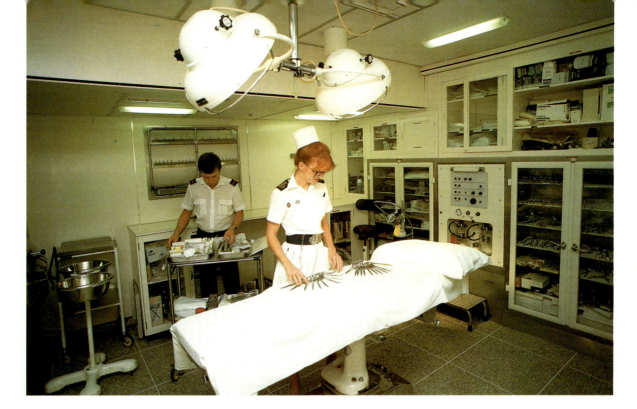

The ship's operating theatre.

is nursed in one of four 3-bed wards, or in the single-bed ward which is used mainly for infectious cases and for those needing intensive care. Should surgery be necessary, there is a fully equipped operating theatre. The hospital is staffed by two doctors, three sisters and three medical attendants.

The laundry

Even on a short cruise, an almost unimaginable amount of laundry is washed and ironed each day. Most of it consists of tablecloths and towels. This is because fresh tablecloths are laid in all restaurants for each meal, and cabins are supplied with clean towels daily.

The laundry workers are on duty long hours each day, although the pace of work changes from frantic bursts of activity to stretches of relative calm. When the dirty laundry does arrive, it is first stuffed into enormous washing machines which can hold up to nearly 400 kilograms at a time. Once it has been washed, it is heaped into baskets and carried over to the pressing machine. The men often do this on the run. They then feed the towels and linen between two enormous rollers. On the other side, two more men fold everything into neat piles. The atmosphere is hot, stuffy and noisy.

Laundry workers at full stretch.

The carpenters' workshop

Repairing a bed.

Few passengers realise how much work is done by the ship's carpenters, electricians and plumbers. Much of the carpenters' time is spent doing repairs. These can be done on site — repairing a passenger's wardrobe, for example — or in the workshop. Some jobs are very simple; others, particularly those involving machines in the engine room, can be more complicated. As always, the carpenters have to try and do as many repairs at sea as possible in order to cut down the amount of time needed in port.

One of the carpenter's more unusual duties is to check the ship's water tanks. The tanks are at the very bottom of the ship and have a variety of uses. One tank holds drinking water; another, the water for washing the laundry — and so on. Some tanks are there just to help keep the ship properly balanced. If, for example, more water were used from one side than another, the ship would begin to lean and more water would have to be pumped into the lower tank to right the ship. It would be the carpenter's duty to make sure this was done. Normally, however, he would correct any slight lean (or list) long before it became apparent to anyone else.

The printer's shop

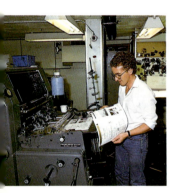

Another programme rolls of the press.

Early each morning, a printed programme of the day's events is delivered to all passenger cabins. So many different activities take place each hour that any attempt to announce them over the loud-speakers would result in chaos. Tucked inside the programme is a daily newsletter. This gives shortened versions of some of the most interesting news stories from around the world. The news items are telexed to the ship by the *Birmingham Post*.

The five printers work in a small room on Six deck. Here they print all the ship's stationery, invitations, memos and menus — as well as 1500 copies of the daily programmes and newsletters. Often they have to work late into the night to make sure everything is ready on time. If things get very busy, they may not see daylight for several days at a stretch.

8
The passengers

The focus of all this planning and hard work is of course, the passengers. If, at the end of the cruise, they leave the ship feeling relaxed and happy, it is quite probable that they will return for another cruise in the future. Cunard know that usually more than 40% of passengers on any cruise have sailed with the *QE2* before. They will also tell their friends and relatives about the trip, and so encourage other people to book a holiday on the ship.

The restaurants

From experience, Cunard knows that most passengers consider good food and wine an important part of a successful cruise. For this reason, a lot of time and effort is spent choosing high-quality ingredients, and employing skilled chefs to cook them. The restaurants too are decorated with care, and staffed with enough waiters to ensure that diners do not have to wait a long time between courses.

At the beginning of a cruise, the passengers are allocated to particular tables which they sit at throughout the voyage. There are normally six or seven people to each table. They are served by two or more waiters, who each look after a maximum of nine passengers. In all four restaurants, the waiters are divided into sections, each of which is looked after by one head waiter. It is the head waiter's job to make sure his group is working smoothly and efficiently.

A good waiter must be master of several skills. First, and most important, he must remember who has ordered what! This is not as

Serving dinner.

easy as it sounds, particularly as people tend to arrive for meals at about the same time. He must also know how to serve an enormous variety of foods with both speed and elegance. Part of a meal's appeal depends on the way in which it is presented. Then, he must be able to judge when to remove one course and serve the next. Too short an interval will make the diner feel rushed; too long an interval will lead to impatience and irritation. Finally, he must always remain polite and friendly, however rushed or bad-tempered he may be feeling inside.

Entertainment

People not only want to be fed well, they also want to be entertained. Otherwise boredom could quickly set in.

On board entertainment takes a variety of forms. During the day, it is mostly informal. People join in organised activities, such as computer-programming lessons, bingo and clay-pigeon shooting, or simply take advantage of the swimming pools, gym and library. In good weather, most people like to spend the day on deck. There are

Sunbathing on Quarter Deck.

two decks to choose from and neither gets very crowded. Older people are happy just to sit in a deckchair and enjoy the fresh air; more active people get their exercise by swimming, jogging or playing deck games. These include deck tennis, miniature golf and quoits, in which players have to throw wooden rings onto a large bullseye painted onto the deck.

The Peter Gordeno Dancers take the floor.

At night, the entertainment is more elaborate. In the Queen's room, the ship's largest public room, the evening begins with an hour-long variety programme. The performers may number singers, comedians, dancers, and instrumentalists. Some are quite well-known, appearing regularly in theatres and on television. 'Big names' help to sell more holidays on the QE2.

A small number of entertainers are employed as crew. Among them are the dancers who introduce the shows each evening. They perform a different dance routine every night. They wear very glamorous costumes. Many are decorated with sequins or feathers, which sparkle and glow under the spotlights. They have a wardrobe of over 360 costumes, which are kept in a small dressing-room behind the stage. Here all six girls have to change and put on their make-up. It is very cramped! Fortunately, after working together for several years the girls know each other well enough not to mind.

The dancers' dressing room.

Excursions

People who decide to have a holiday on the *QE2* usually do so because they want to experience life on board a luxury ship. Where the ship goes is of less importance. Nevertheless, once the *QE2* has docked in an unfamiliar place, most passengers like to go ashore to do some sightseeing.

Unlike most American passengers, the British are unadventurous travellers and are wary of exploring on their own. For them in particular, Cunard arranges a series of guided tours. These range from a short walk around the nearest town, to a day-long coach trip to the main local sights. The organisation of the tours is handled in London or New York, several months before the cruise starts. But minor details often have to be changed by staff on board the *QE2*.

One stopping-off place which regularly appears on the *QE2*'s European cruise itinerary is Gibraltar. Although situated at the southern tip of Spain, Gibraltar belongs to Britain and is a popular destination with British travellers. The main town is built at the foot of a

A first view of Gibraltar.

A Barbary ape.

huge flat-topped rock. The streets are narrow and winding, and are lined with little shops selling duty-free goods. Halfway up the rock lives a colony of Barbary apes. The apes have become one of Gibraltar's main tourist attractions. It is said that when the apes leave Gibraltar, the British will leave too. But there seems little chance of this as a keeper has been appointed to make sure the apes are always well fed!

Home and away

As each cruise draws to an end, the passengers start thinking of home. On the last evening, they pack their suitcases and leave them in the corridor outside their cabins. During the night, the stewards will carry them to the gangway exits, ready for collection by porters on shore. Before then, there is one more dinner on ship. As people eat, they talk about their days at sea. For many, the cruise is already beginning to seem unreal. Tomorrow, when they drive back onto the busy, noisy roads, it will feel almost like a dream.

Early next morning, the ship arrives in Southampton. After breakfast, the passengers wait in the lounges to disembark. The crew, meanwhile, are working hard. The stewards and stewardesses strip and make all the passengers' beds and clean their cabins. The restaurant and kitchen staff clear the dining rooms, the cleaners hoover and dust all the stairways and corridors, and the laundry workers wash and press hundreds of sheets and towels.

Outside on the quay, the dock workers are loading fresh supplies of food on board. They started two hours ago, at 7 o'clock. The vans and lorries contain enough food and drink for an 11-day round trip to New York. The ship will only spend five hours at New York so most supplies have to be taken on board in Southampton. Loading must be completed by 5 p.m. At 3 p.m. the first America-bound passengers will start to arrive. Until then a few lucky members of crew may spend some hours ashore. The rest will snatch a nap in their cabins. At 7 o'clock, the *QE2* will embark on a transatlantic crossing, and another five days of hard work will begin.

Back in Southampton dock.

Index

Facts and figures

(to the nearest round figure)

Gross tonnage (total weight of freight which can be transported at one time): 68,216 tonnes

Overall length: 293 metres   **Breadth**: 32 metres

Height (keel to funnel base): 38 metres   (keel to masthead): 62 metres   **Number of decks**: 13

Deck space: 3,763 square metres   **Passenger lifts**: 24

Crew: 995   **Service speed**: $28\frac{1}{2}$ knots (53 kms per hour)

Propellers: 2 (6-bladed)